CW01665963

OBSERVING THE RAILWAY in 2024

A pictorial review of the year

RCTS PUBLICATIONS

www.rcts.org.uk

ISBN 978-1-7391324-9-1

Published by The Railway Correspondence and Travel Society,
16 Welby Close, Maidenhead SL6 3PY, United Kingdom.

Printed in the Czech Republic via Akcent Media Limited

Typesetting and page layout by RCTS Members.

FOREWORD

In this book we present a photographic record of the contemporary railway scene on the national rail network during 2024 using pictures taken by the members of the Railway Correspondence & Travel Society (RCTS). It covers locations from Cornwall to the north of Scotland and from East Anglia to South Wales, with a mix of rural and built-up areas. The new trains introduced in the year and older ones taken out of service are featured as well as some of the special liveries applied to both locomotives and multiple units. Full page, high-quality images are backed-up by informative captions and are presented month-by-month in date order.

LEFT

Diverted because of engineering works on the Swansea District line, DB Cargo Class 66s 66007 and 66053, which was still in EWS livery, head the 13.53 Theale-Robeston discharged tanks through Llansamlet on a sunny Tuesday 18th June.

Stephen Miles

FRONT COVER

Colas Class 70 70816, with the diverted 6M40 Westbury Yard-Cliffe Hill Stud Farm, was passing Stourbridge Junction on Wednesday 21st August.

Steve Burdett

REAR COVER

CAF Class 196/1 Civity four-car DMU 196102 arrives at Great Malvern with the West Midlands Trains 13.50 Birmingham New St.-Hereford on Friday 10th May.

Stewart Leyland

INTRODUCTION

Between January and March 2024 there was a 13% increase in passenger journeys compared with the previous year though this was still less than pre-pandemic levels, at 91% relative to the same quarter five years ago in 2019. TransPennine Express had a 38% increase largely a result of the increase in trains planned compared with the reduced timetables in place in 2023.

The improvement continued in the June quarter with an increase of 7% with just three days of industrial action, followed by 9% increase in the September quarter, with TransPennine Express again leading the way with a 25% rise. The year ended with another 7% increase in the quarter ended December with journeys almost the same as in 2019.

The total volume of freight moved fell by 5% in the first quarter of 2024 compared with 2023 but recovered for the remainder of the year with successive quarterly increases of 7%, 2% and 6%. The composition of the traffic changed with coal phased out as a supplementary source of power for the National Grid and replaced by biomass. The generators at Drax were all converted by the end of the year producing higher rail volumes from Immingham and Liverpool and Lynemouth came online in 2024.

Intermodal non-maritime increased by 79% and 89% in the first two quarters with smaller gains in the final two quarters of 11% and 14% as use of rail by retailers such as Tesco and by manufacturers like Coca Cola increased. Intermodal maritime fell in the first quarter to its lowest level since 2010 but recovered during the remainder of the year, and construction followed a similar pattern.

In December the government confirmed the timescales for the first three train operators (SWR, c2c and Greater Anglia) to transfer to the public sector following royal assent to the Passenger Railway Services (Public Ownership) Act 2024 which provides the legal framework.

Several new stations were opened during the year and the passenger service between Newcastle and Ashington was restored In December, 60 years after it was withdrawn by British Railways.

Several new classes came into service during the year with Avanti West Coast introducing the Hitachi Class 805 bi-mode in June and the Hitachi Class 807 EMU in November. In South Wales the TfW 756 tri-mode entered service in November followed in December by the first new Class 555 on the Tyneside Metro.

The introduction of Class 720 EMUs by Greater Anglia continued with almost all of them in service by the end of the year, and more Class 730 EMUs and Class 197 DMUs entered traffic with West Midlands Trains.

One blackspot was on South Western Trains whose Class 701 Arterios finally entered service in January, over four years late, but only five were in operation by the end of the year. It is still uncertain how long it will be before the 90 sets ordered are in use.

The final demise of the Merseyrail Class 507 and 508 EMUs came in the middle of the year and Royal Mail terminated its postal contract in October resulting in the withdrawal of the Class 325 units.

However, the shortened HST sets continued to work at both ends of the country, on ScotRail and on the GWR although the latter will be replaced by former Transport for Wales Class 175s. The Class 60s enjoyed a renaissance on DC Rail with two more due to return to traffic in 2025 and GB Railfreight re-introduced them on its stone traffic in addition to their regular use on biomass trains to Drax power station.

ACKNOWLEDGMENTS

This book would not have been possible without the time spent in all types of weather at the lineside by the following: Tony Bartlett, Steve Batty, Steve Burdett, Paul Chancellor, David Cox, Richard Davies, Peter Fogarty, Bob Hayes, Derek Huntriss, Graham Jelly, John Jennison, Stewart Jolly, Jack Kernahan, Julien King, Stewart Leyland, Rodney Lissenden, Darren Martin, Stephen Miles, Bernard Mills, Keith Partlow, Ian Pilkington, Chris Powell, Mike Robinson, Graham Roose, Keith Sanders, John Sloane, Richard Vitler and Stuart Warr.

John Jennison, Editor

CONTENTS

On a Saturday working, GB Railfreight Class 66/7 66740 *Sarah* heads north with a North Blyth to Fort William alumina train (6S45). It was passing Peelwalls in the Scottish Borders (between Ayton and Reston), on 18th May. 66740 was purchased by GBRf from Freightliner in March 2011, renumbered from 66580 and named in August 2014 after Sarah Whurr who worked in the GBRf finance team.

Keith Sanders

The Transport for Wales Class 230 battery-electric hybrid multiple units, rebuilt from London Underground stock, make a curious sight operating along the Welsh Borders Wrexham-Bidston route. Although their reliability had improved, only one set operated each day, with the other diagrams on the line covered by Class 197 units. On Wednesday 3rd January, 230007 was waiting at Wrexham Central ready to depart to Bidston. TfW modified its Class 230 fleet during the year to improve reliability. Battery issues were traced to the diesel generators not producing high power during acceleration, causing the batteries to overwork. By early 2025 the units were working two all-day diagrams with Class 197s working one diagram; the aim is to increase this to three.

Darren Martin

Colas Class 56s, 56049 *Robin of Templecombe* and 56113 power away from Hellifield on Thursday 4th January with the 12.52 Carlisle Yard-Chirk Kronospan loaded timber carriers. There was a regular traffic of timber each week to the Kronospan wood processing factory at Chirk, south of Wrexham, both from Carlisle and, until the end of the year, from Baglan Bay in South Wales. *Chris Powell*

Merseyrail Class 777 Stadler four-car EMU 777012 departs from Chester on Wednesday 10th January with the 14.15 service to Liverpool Central via Hooton and Birkenhead Central. The 17.65 miles-long journey was scheduled to take 45 minutes with 16 intermediate stops. After a wait at Liverpool of less than a minute the unit will return to Chester arriving at 15.40 and five minutes later will repeat the journey. *Chris Powell*

Among the oldest units still operating on the network, BR York-built Class 150/1 Sprinter two-car DMU 150134 operated by Northern, departs from Chester on Wednesday 10th January with the 13.56 service to Manchester Piccadilly via Northwich and Altrincham. This unit was built in January 1986 at BREL York and has a Cummins 285hp engine driving a Voith hydraulic transmission on each car. *Chris Powell*

Northern Class 195 CAF Civity three-car DMUs 195128 and 195111 wait at Preston on Wednesday 10th January with the 08.29 Manchester Airport-Windermere service.
Chris Powell

The 'New Order' on the Rhymney branch on Friday 12th January as Transport for Wales' Class 231 Stadler FLIRT diesel-electric four-car unit 231003 slows for a brief stop at Ystrad Mynach whilst working the 10.18 Penarth-Bargoed. *Stuart Warr*

On a cold Monday 15th January Transport for Wales Class 197 CAF Civity two-car DMU 197011 was working the 1D37 12.25 Manchester Airport-Llandudno when crossing over the River Weaver Navigation at Frodsham. *Stewart Leyland*

Merseyrail Class 777 Stadler four-car EMU 777026 was about to leave the Grade II listed station at Ellesmere Port with the 14.42 round trip to Liverpool and back on Monday 15th January. The service via Birkenhead and Rock Ferry runs every 30 minutes and calls at all three Liverpool stations, Lime Street, Central and James Street, and takes around 80 minutes for the 26-mile journey. *Stewart Leyland*

On Monday 15th January GB Railfreight's sole Class 59, 59003 *Yeoman Highlander*, was leaving a busy Eastleigh yard on the afternoon trip to Westbury, with two Class 08 shunters and a Class 66 in the yard. *Darren Martin*

Lumo Class 803 Hitachi five-car EMU 803003 with Pride vinyls passed through Peterborough on Wednesday 17th January working the 09.24 Edinburgh-Kings Cross. A report published in February 2025 found that Lumo, one of First Group's two open access operators, had helped to generate more than six million new rail journeys, encouraging people to switch from air travel to rail. *Keith Partlow*

Storm Isha crossed the UK overnight on 21st/22nd January, and on the Heart of Wales line eight trees were blown onto the track. Following their clearance a 'proving run' was operated on Monday 22nd as 5V06, the Transport for Wales 08.57 Shrewsbury-Swansea running in the place of the similarly timed service train. It used a pair of TfW Class 153 single units, 153914 and 153362, which were photographed passing slowly through Pantyffynnon. The Class 153s were converted in 1991/2 from Regional Railways Class 155 two-car units. 153914 was renumbered from 153314 in 2020 because it had a non-compliant toilet under a new regulation 'Persons with Reduced Mobility - Technical Specifications' signifying that it had to work attached to a Class 153/3 or Class 150/2 unit, unless the overall journey was quite short. *Stuart Warr*

Viewed from the platform at Upholland station on Monday 22nd January, two Northern Class 150/1 Sprinter DMUs, led by 150136, approach on a working from Blackburn via Rochdale and Manchester to Headbolt Lane, the interchange at Kirkby with the Merseyrail northern line. Upholland tunnel with its prominent ventilation shaft looms in the background. *John Sloane*

A TransPennine moment at Manchester Oxford Road on Wednesday 24th January when Class 397 EMU 397004 called with a Manchester Airport to Edinburgh Waverley service whilst another unidentified Class 397 waited with a service in the opposite direction. *John Sloane*

DCR Class 60 60055 *Thomas Barnado* comes out of March Down Yard on Wednesday 24th January working the 14.11 Brandon-Chaddesden empty boxes. Devon & Cornwall Rail Freight has been a national rail freight operator since 2011, and part of the Cappagh Group of Companies and it purchased 60055 from DB Schenker in 2019. However, the locomotive remained in store at Toton until returned to service in March 2022 after extensive repairs. *Keith Partlow*

Hinksey Yard, south of Oxford, continues to be busy as a virtual quarry and general staging point for engineering trains. On Monday 29th January. Class 66111, still in EWS livery, was stabled in the yard as Class 70 70001 headed north on the main line with a Freightliner train from Southampton. 70001, built at General Electric at their Erie, Pennsylvania plant in the USA, was the first of GE's successor to their 3,300hp Class 66s using the more powerful Powerhaul P616LDA1 3,820hp engine and entered service in late 2009. *Darren Martin*

A sunny Thursday, the first day of February, made the yellow Ukraine-liveried LNwR Class 350 Siemens Desiro four-car EMU 350104 look even brighter as it departed from Wolverhampton with the 09.33 Liverpool Lime Street-Birmingham New Street. *Steve Burdett*

TransPennine Express Class 68 Stadler 68027 *Splendid* passes through Wolverhampton with 5Q94 from Longsight TMD on Thursday 1st February conveying displaced TransPennine Express Nova 3 stock to Long Marston for storage. 68027 was one of the 14 Class 68s which were sub-leased by TPE from Direct Rail Services and were handed back to Beacon Rail at the end of their leases in May. *Steve Burdett*

The ever-growing skyline of central Manchester provides the background for two East Midlands Railway Class 170 Turbostars, 170206 in EMR Regional two-tone grey livery and 170203 in aubergine, as they approached Oxford Road station on Thursday 1st February with a Liverpool Lime Street to Norwich service.
John Sloane

East Midlands Railway trains briefly dominated Manchester Oxford Road station on Thursday 1st February as services between Liverpool Lime Street and Norwich made simultaneous calls. The westbound service comprised units Class 158 Express Sprinters 158889 and 158774 whilst Class 170 Turbostar 170203 was at the rear of the Norwich-bound service. *John Sloane*

Direct Rail Services Class 68 Stadler 3,755hp Bo-Bos 68018 *Vigilant* and 68002 *Intrepid* pass through Ipswich on Friday 2nd February working the 13.30 Sizewell-Willesden Brent conveying one wagon carrying a nuclear flask. *Keith Partlow*

GB Railfreight Class 66/7 66744 *Crossrail* at Foxton on Wednesday 7th February working the 11.57 Barrington Pad-Willesden Euroterminal empty boxes. Three trains per day ran to Barrington GBRf discharge pads conveying spoil from HS2 for tipping into the former limestone pits at the erstwhile Barrington cement works. They reversed into the exchange sidings from Foxton station on the Cambridge to Royston line and then ran round. The inbound loaded working waited for the empties to come up the branch before completing the short journey to the pad. The discharged trains departed directly to Cambridge before running round and continuing south over the Lea Valley route back to Willesden. *Keith Partlow*

Two of the rapidly declining number of Class 507 units at Southport on Thursday 8th February. The first of the class, 507001, repainted in heritage blue and grey livery, after arrival from Hunts Cross was alongside 507029 in the yellow Merseyrail livery. *John Sloane*

South Western Railway Class 450 Desiro EMUs 450114 and 450048 enter Windsor & Eton Riverside station with a service from Waterloo on Friday 9th February. The station was opened in December 1849 by the London & South Western Railway and a Royal waiting room, given Grade II listing in 1975, was added in 1851. It enjoys a half-hourly service in each direction with a journey time of around 55 minutes for the 25.48-mile journey. This was the first service to be worked by the new Class 701s when they finally made their debut the previous month. *Stewart Leyland*

GB Railfreight Class 66/7 66707 *Sir Sam Fay* runs alongside the New Cut at Haddiscoe on Thursday 15th February working the 6P52 12.13 Whitemoor-Lowestoft empty boxes. *Keith Partlow*

Railway Support Services Class 08, 08507 at Whitemoor on Friday 16th February shunting GB Railfreight Class 66/7 66792 *Collaboration* and a rake of Autoballasters. Whitemoor yards are a shadow of their heyday; decline set in from the early 1960s as wagonload traffic reduced although Whitemoor continued as a marshalling yard into 1980, but then lay dormant until 2004, when a phased reintroduction of the site began. The marshalling yard re-opened, and in 2011 a recycling plant was constructed on the site of the Up Departure Sidings by Network Rail to handle used ballast, track panels, sleepers, rails, small steel components and switches and crossings units. The materials are graded and sorted into what can be reused on the network and what can be sold on to external organisations such as the construction industry. 08507 was built as D3662 in 1958 and was purchased by Harry Needle Railroad Company after withdrawal and was sold to RSS in 2022; it was at Whitemoor from June 2023 until April 2024.

Keith Partlow

Great Western Railway Class 43 Castle, 43098 *Walton Castle* at the rear of the 12.50 Penzance-Plymouth departing from Lostwithiel on Friday 16th February. To the right is the new colour light signal on the Down platform which allows direct access, mainly for the Carne Point clay empties, to run into the Down loop for reversal purposes. This came into use a month later when the signal box closed, and the area was taken over by the Exeter Panel and all of the semaphores were removed. *Bernard Mills*

On Saturday 24th February, GWR Castle class HST 43093 *Berkeley Castle* arrives at Par station with a Plymouth to Penzance service. The semaphore signals were swept away two weeks later when the new signalling came into operation. *Peter Fogarty*

Ex-Northern Class 150/2 Sprinter 150207, built at BREL York in May 1987, passes through Hungerford on Monday 4th March. It was destined for service with GWR after a 'makeover' by Gemini at Wolverton Works, and was on delivery to Exeter, for later deployment on services in Devon and Cornwall. A Freightliner Class 66-hauled stone train was about to pass in the opposite direction, reflected in the DMU cab window.

Tony Bartlett

Recently transferred and still in its West Midlands livery, Class 323 EMU 323220 was stabled at Wigan North Western station on Wednesday 6th March awaiting what was probably a crew familiarisation working prior to entering service with Northern. The first Hunslet-built Class 323 was introduced in February 1994 and the West Midlands allocation totalled 25 units, entering full service the following year and another 18 units were built for use on routes radiating from Manchester. As the West Midlands Railway fleet was replaced by new Class 730s during the year, its Class 323s were cascaded to augment the fleet in the north west inherited by Northern. *John Sloane*

Trains from both of First Group's open access operators wait for departure at London Kings Cross on Monday 11th March. In the foreground Hull Trains Class 802/3 Paragon Hitachi bi-mode 802303 *Land of Green Ginger* formed the 11.48 to Hull while Lumo Class 803 Hitachi five-car EMU 803003 would follow with the 12.18 to Edinburgh. *Chris Powell*

Northern Class 333 CAF four-car EMU 333014 at Kirkstall Forge on Wednesday 13th March with the 15.03 Leeds-Ilkley service. Kirkstall Forge station was opened in 2016 and serves the local community as well as being a park and ride station for Leeds. It is served by Leeds-Bradford Forster Square services but at this date Leeds-Ilkley services were also stopping here to provide connections to Bradford as the line between Guiseley and Shipley was closed due to a major landslip at Baildon.

Chris Powell

South Western Railway Bombardier Class 701 Arterio EMU 701003 during a proving run from Waterloo to Poole and back to Staines passing through Eastleigh on Wednesday 13th March. The first of the 90, long-delayed Class 701s entered revenue earning service on 9th January but only five Arterios were in service by the end of the year. *John Sloane*

GB Railfreight Class 66/3 66307 *Ipswich Town* leaves Whitemoor Yard on Friday 15th March working the 12.13 empty IOA boxes for Lowestoft. The IOA is a type of high sided wagon introduced in 2009 designed to carry ballast and spoil and with a maximum load capacity of 102 tonnes.

Keith Partlow

Over a few days in mid-March the line between Wigan Wallgate and Southport was closed for track renewal work west of Parbold. On Monday 18th March Freightliner Powerhaul-liveried Class 66 66504 had arrived at Parbold from Crewe Basford Hall with a rake of empty spoil wagons. After reversing over the crossover the train was hand signalled to run wrong line across the level crossing in order to reach the works site further west near Hoscar. *John Sloane*

Southeastern Bombardier Class 376 Electrostar five-car EMU 376007 calls at London Bridge with the 15.11 Orpington-Cannon Street on a busy Saturday 30th March. The 36 high-capacity Class 376s were built in 2004/5 for use on the inner suburban routes running from Central London to Kent. Each car has two sets of double doors per side; these were wide to allow more passengers to board at once, and with sliding pocket rather than plug doors. They have fewer seats and more handrails to provide additional standing room. *John Sloane*

The Shard building looms over the rebuilt London Bridge station as Class 376 Electrostar EMU 376005 arrives with the Southeastern 15.31 from Charing Cross to Maidstone East on Saturday 30th March. In the latest figures published in November 2024, London Bridge was the seventh busiest station in the country with 50 million passenger entries and exits in 2023/24. *John Sloane*

Northern Class 195/1 CAF Civity three-car DMU 195115 departs from Church Fenton on Thursday 4th April with the 12.24 York-Blackpool North. Church Fenton is around 10¾ miles south of York and is the junction between the York-Leeds line and the Dearne Valley line from Sheffield.

Chris Powell

On Sunday 7th April, Chiltern Railways Class 165/0 Networker Turbo two-car DMUs 165038 and 165006 depart from Wembley Stadium station after bringing in Wycombe Wanderers Football Club fans on a special service from High Wycombe for the Bristol Street Motors EFL Trophy final against Peterborough United which they lost 2-1. Note Wembley TMD in the right background of the photograph. *Peter Fogarty*

Elizabeth Line Bombardier Class 345 Aventra nine-car EMU 345059 calls at Acton Main Line station with a Heathrow to Abbey Wood service on Thursday 11th April. The 30.4-mile journey takes just over an hour inclusive of 16 stops. The Aventras are of lightweight construction and have full-width gangways and mainly longitudinal seating like modern Underground stock. Each car has three pairs of bi-parting sliding doors to facilitate rapid loading and unloading. The Elizabeth Line now carries more than 700,000 people every day. *John Sloane*

The level crossing at Oakham in Rutland crosses a major intersection in the centre of the town. While the crossing, signalling and motive power have been upgraded many times, the 1899 Midland Railway Type 2b signal box remains constant. On the afternoon of Thursday 11th April GB Railfreight Class 66/7 66778 *Cambois Depot 25 Years* was heading a lengthy container train through the town bound for Felixstowe. The signal box was given Grade II listing in 1990 and achieved fame as the prototype for the Airfix OO scale model kit which was first released in 1957 and is still on sale today from the Dapol model company.
Darren Martin

Bombardier Class 378/2 Capitalstar five-car EMU 378205 which had the colourful LGBTQ+ 'Every Story matters' Pride livery arrives at Highbury & Islington with a service to Stratford on Friday 12th April. In contrast to years past, Highbury & Islington is now an important and busy interchange between the Underground and Overground systems and it enjoys extensive connections across London. *John Sloane*

The main line out of Euston appears quiet as Class 710/3 Aventra 710378 passed Northwick Park at Kenton with a working from Watford heading for Euston on Friday 12th April. Six of these Bombardier five-car dual-voltage EMUs were ordered by Transport for London in 2017 for the North and West London lines and they began operation between Euston and Watford in September 2019. *John Sloane*

Greater Anglia Class 745/1 Stadler FLIRT twelve-car Stansted Express EMU 745104 was about to sweep through Romford with the 11.30 from Liverpool Street to Norwich on Friday 12th April. To the right, a Class 345 Aventra EMU is arriving with the 12.07 Elizabeth line service from Paddington to Shenfield. A pleasing feature here is the provision of some pseudo-Eastern Region pattern blue station signs with white uppercase lettering.

Graham Jelly

Avanti West Coast Class 805 Evero five-car bi-mode 805009 races past South Kenton with a Euston to Edge Hill mileage accumulation working on Friday 12th April, before the first of these units entered traffic in June. They were built for services between London, Birmingham and Holyhead to replace the Class 221 Voyager DMUs which were all transferred away by the end of the year.

John Sloane

Pending electrification of the East Kilbride branch the monopoly of Class 156 DMUs at Pollokshaws West is broken only by one electric service each hour between Glasgow Central and Barrhead. Class 380/1 Siemens Desiro four-car EMU 380112 called there with the 11.57 from Glasgow on Tuesday 16th April. *Jack Kernahan*

The days of Transport for Wales Class 158 Express Sprinter DMUs on Cambrian Coast line duties were numbered by the middle of the year with trials of Civity Class 197s being undertaken. The BR Derby-built units entered service between 1990 and 1992 to replace loco-hauled trains on longer-distance services. TfW Class 158/8 two-car unit 158825 arrives at Harlech with the 10.55 Machynlleth-Pwllheli on Thursday 18th April.

Steve Burdett

Class 350 Siemens Desiro four-car EMU 350119 waiting to depart from Wolverhampton with the West Midlands Trains 11.33 Liverpool Lime Street-Birmingham New Street on Saturday 20th April.

John Jennison

In 2021 ScotRail introduced its Highland Explorer service which uses Class 153 single units modified to take up to twenty cycles and associated gear on the West Highland Line between Glasgow and Oban. Initially a £10 supplement was charged but this was dropped in 2023. 153380 brings up the rear of an Oban to Glasgow Queen Street service at Dalmally on Sunday 28th April. The lead unit was Class 156 Super Sprinter two-car 156453. According to the staff at Oban the Class 153s are popular with visitors. *Stewart Leyland*

ScotRail Class 156 Super Sprinter two-car 156508 waits at Ayr on Wednesday 1st May. The building in the background covered by tarpaulins is the south wing of the former Station Hotel. The 1885-built Grade-B listed building was abandoned after it closed in 2012 and deteriorated steadily until September 2023 when an arson attack left it in an unsafe condition which resulted in electric trains from Glasgow terminating at Prestwick and a two-car DMU shuttle between Ayr and Prestwick was introduced to replace the EMUs. Demolition of the remains of the building had started earlier in the year but was delayed by a legal challenge from its Malaysian owner. This was dismissed by the Scottish Court of Session on 3rd May and work was completed in June when electric services to Glasgow resumed. *Mike Robinson*

With McCaig's Tower in the background, ScotRail Class 156 Super Sprinter two-car 156456 after arrival at Oban with the 1Y21 from Glasgow Queen Street on Wednesday 1st May. The 101-mile journey which takes over three hours places a heavy demand on the Class 156s which are now almost forty years old. *Stewart Leyland*

TransPennine Express Class 802/2 bi-mode 802214 passes Church Fenton on Thursday 2nd May with the 14.43 Newcastle-Liverpool Lime Street while in the background Northern Class 155 155345 arrives with the 15.46 York-Bridlington via Hull. Nineteen of the five-car sets were built by Hitachi in 2018/19 for TransPennine Express services between Edinburgh/Newcastle and Liverpool/Manchester. *Chris Powell*

Ex-Transport for Wales Class 175 Coradia DMUs 175110 and 175011 pass through March station on Thursday 9th May working as 5Q46 the 11.17 Crewe South Yard-Ely Papworth for storage. They were replaced by new Class 197s with all the Class 175s taken out of service by the end of 2023. The fleet has now been leased from Angel Trains by GWR with the first unit delivered to Laira on 27th November 2024 and will enter service during 2025. *Keith Partlow*

Class 60s have begun to appear on workings out of Rylstone quarry. On Thursday 9th May GB Railfreight Class 60 60096 *Impetus* lifts the 18.20 Rylstone Quarry-Hull Dairycoates loaded aggregates hoppers past Taylor's Bridge near Rylstone Village. 60096 was built by Brush in 1992 and carried the name *Ben Macdui* for its first decade in service. It was sold by DB Schenker to Colas Rail in 2014 who sold it on to GBRf in 2018 and it was then named *Impetus*. In May 2024 it received another mountain name when it was renamed *Skiddaw* with Class 44 Peak style 1960s nameplates.
Chris Powell

A multi-million-pound renovation at the Grade II listed Great Malvern station in which the ornate Victorian platform canopies were repaired, reglazed and repainted was completed in December 2023. Class 196/1 CAF Civity four-car DMU 196102 arrived there with West Midlands Trains 13.50 Birmingham New Street-Hereford on Friday 10th May. *Stewart Leyland*

If staying at the Premier Inn in Worcester and using the Realtime Trains app, this location can be photographed between courses. During breakfast on Saturday 11th May Great Western Railway Class 800 Hitachi five-car bi-mode 800030 was crossing the River Severn whilst working the 06.50 Paddington-Great Malvern. *Stewart Leyland*

DB Cargo Class 66/6 66651, formerly 66221, was the first of ten DB Class 66s to be re-geared as replacements for withdrawn Class 60s; it returned to service after modification on 13th April. The modifications which were carried out at Toton depot produced an increase of 14% in tractive effort and the work also included repainting, new wheelsets, and LED headlights. On Monday 13th May 66651 was at work hauling the Wilton-Knowsley empty binliner train through the cutting at Orrell station. *John Sloane*

GWR Class 800 Hitachi five-car bi-mode 800002 arrives at Evesham with the 13.16 Worcester Shrub Hill to London Paddington service on Wednesday 15th May. This train had suffered a slight delay due to a bicycle on the line!

Steve Burdett

Transport for Wales Class 158 Express Sprinter two-car DMU 158836 working the 08.52 Machynlleth- Pwllheli on Friday 17th May had just crossed the Afon Mawddach (River Mawddach) over the Barmouth bridge and was preparing to stop at Barmouth station. It had emerged from the unusual short seventy yards-long tunnel which has above a cutting through which a road passed and was about to cross the 78 yards-long, six-span viaduct 'Old Chapel Viaduct' ; the original wooden structure here had been rebuilt in concrete in 1952. *Stuart Warr*

After a very short turn around at Sheerness-on-Sea on the Isle of Sheppey, Southeastern Class 375/3 Electrostar three-car EMU 375308 was about to embark on the 11-mile, part single track, journey back to Sittingbourne with the 12.47 Southeastern service on Monday 20th May. Apart from the loss of the centre siding, this platform view is fairly timeless.
Graham Jelly

With the closure of Lostwithiel signal box under the March 2024 resignalling scheme, a new token platform was constructed on the Carne Point (formerly Fowey) branch, about 200 yards down from the main line junction at Coulson Park beside the River Fowey. Here, control from the workstation at Exeter Panel ends and the train had to stop for the driver to alight to contact Exeter for the release of the token for the branch. DB Cargo Class 66/0 66101 was ready to proceed with the 12.36 Goonbarrow Junction-Carne Point on Monday 20th May. This train now only runs on Mondays, Tuesdays and Wednesdays. *Bernard Mills*

Tonbridge is a good location to view freight activity. GB Railfreight Class 66/7 66751 *Inspirational Delivered Hitachi Rail Europe* passed through with 7Z11 Hoo Junction-Tonbridge Yard on Friday 24th May. The name was bestowed on 66751 in April 2015 "to celebrate the relationship between GB Railfreight and Hitachi Rail Europe" in advance of its use to haul Hitachi's Class 800 pre-series train on the East Coast Main Line.

Steve Burdett

With its unique livery standing out in the sunshine, Direct Rail Services Class 88 Stadler bi-mode 88010 *Aurora* heads north at Docker on Saturday 1st June with the 06.40 Daventry-Mossend Tesco Express container train, a regular working for the ten Class 88s since their introduction in 2017. 88010 received the half-blue, half frozen livery with the slogan 'Refrigerated Rail ...COOL Move' in July 2022 "to promote the transport of refrigerated goods by rail". *Chris Powell*

Alsager in Cheshire has had a station since 1848 when it was opened by the North Staffordshire Railway on its line between Crewe and Stoke-on-Trent. An East Midlands Railway service, the 14.10 from Crewe to Newark Castle in the hands of Class 158 Express Sprinter two-car DMU 158863 called there on Monday 3rd June. The line between Crewe and Kidsgrove was electrified in 2003 to provide a diversionary route during engineering work on the West Coast Main Line. *Steve Burdett*

The tree-lined surroundings belie the fact that Avanti West Coast Evero bi-mode unit 805005 was about to pass through Wigan North Western station during the course of a mileage accumulation/familiarity working on electric power from Wembley Central to Preston on Tuesday 4th June. The first two units had entered service two days earlier, working between Euston and Holyhead. Together with the electric Class 807 Everos, they will replace Avanti's Class 221 Super Voyagers.
John Sloane

On Wednesday 5th June, under Bournemouth's magnificent overall roof, CrossCountry Class 220 Voyager DMUs 220004 and 220026 were arriving with the 07.25 CrossCountry service from Manchester Piccadilly. The 256-mile journey via Birmingham and Oxford took almost five hours. On the left, South Western Railways' Class 444 Siemens Desiro 444021, having arrived from Poole, awaited the Weymouth portion before combining to form the 12.22 to London Waterloo.

Graham Jelly

On Sunday 9th June Cross Country Class 221 Super Voyager 221119 arrives on time at platform 5 at Crewe with the 08.26 from Manchester Piccadilly to Leamington Spa, which it would reach on time.

John Jennison

A pair of Transport for Wales Class 197 CAF Civity DMUs, two-car 197001 and three-car 197103, had arrived exactly on time at Crewe with the 07.46 from Bangor on Sunday 9th June. After 197103 had departed with the TfW 09.22 to Bangor, 197001 moves out from platform 9. On the far right, Direct Rail Services Class 57 Thunderbird 57308 *Jamie Ferguson* stands in the engine siding between platforms 11 and 12.

John Jennison

When an extra platform was added at Stockport it needed to be numbered 0 in order to avoid renumbering all the other platforms. On Monday 10th June, platform 0 was host to the 13.51 East Midlands Railway service from Liverpool Lime Street to Norwich which was worked by a pair of Class 158 Express Sprinter two-car DMUs with 158812 leading. *John Sloane*

On Tuesday 11th June, Cross Country Class 220 Voyager four-car DMU 220032 waits for departure from Sheffield with the 06.28 from Penzance to Edinburgh, where it arrived on time. On the left, Northern Class 195 CAF Civity two-car DMU 195016 departs with the 12.17 from Nottingham to Leeds. *John Jennison*

After bringing 2,000 tonnes of biomass from Port of Tyne to Drax power station, GB Railfreight Brush Class 60 60026 *Helvellyn* was ready to depart with the empties back to Port of Tyne on Monday 17th June. There are 24 scheduled workings from the port to Drax each week. 60026 was built for EWS in 1990 and was named *William Caxton* until 1996; it was sold to Colas Rail in in 2013 and then to GBRf in 2018 when it was given the name *Jupiter* which lasted only a year, until it received its third name, *Helvellyn*, carried on red-backed 1960s style nameplates as used on Class 44 Peak D2.

Paul Chancellor

The new, accessible station footbridge at Taff's Well was almost complete in this view taken on Monday 17th June from the original footbridge. Following the June 2024 timetable change, services on the Merthyr and Aberdare branches have been worked contiguously, running from one terminus to the other via a 'loop' through Cardiff. Transport for Wales Class 150 Sprinter two-car DMU 150237 was departing with the 14.08 Merthyr Tydfil-Cardiff Central-Aberdare, a journey which took slightly over two hours with no fewer than 29 stops! *Stewart Jolly*

South Western Railway Alstom Class 458/5 Juniper EMUs 458532 and 458514 arrive at Clapham Junction's platform 4 with the 06.39 Reading to Waterloo on Friday 21st June. 28 of the five-car Class 458s were in the process of being refurbished by Alstom and reduced to four cars although 458532 was not one of them; along with five others it was built using five heavily refurbished vehicles from withdrawn Class 460 Gatwick Express units. 458514 was one of the original four-car Class 458s and became a 458/5 when refurbished and an additional ex-Class 460 car added; when converted back to a four-car unit by removing the Class 460 car it was renumbered as 458414; the refurbishment work on the fleet was completed by the end of 2024. On the left, South Western Railway Class 450 Siemens Desiro 450005 was about to leave with a down service. *Richard Vitler*

West Midlands Trains Class 196/0 CAF Civity two-car DMUs 196007 and 196001 depart from Malvern Link on Friday 28th June with the 15.39 Hereford-Birmingham New Street. WMT has 12 two-car units of the Rolls-Royce-powered Class 196s and 14 four-car units. *Chris Powell*

On a grey Monday 1st July ScotRail Class 43 43015 had just arrived at Glasgow Queen Street with the 1T84 from Inverness. In the distance, 43147 was slowing into platform 7 with the early arriving 1T26 from Aberdeen. The arrival of two HSTs at Queen Street within the space of ten minutes is unlikely to continue for much longer. 27 sets were cascaded from Great Western Railway after they were replaced by Class 800s; they were refurbished and fitted with plug automatic doors. *Stewart Leyland*

ScotRail Class 318 three-car EMU 318257 at High Street Glasgow on the North Clyde line which passes through Queen Street Low Level with the 08.08 Balloch-Airdrie on Monday 1st July. The fleet of 21 ageing Class 318s were built by BREL York in 1985/86 and have been refurbished three times, the last of which were completed in late 2023.
Stewart Leyland

Rail Operations Group Class 37/7 37884 *Cepheus* passes Wymondham South Junction signal box on Monday 1st July working the 12.32 Ely Papworth-Norwich Crown Point hauling seven ex-GWR Mark 3 coaches sandwiched between Mark 2 barrier coaches 6346 and 6330. 37884 was built by English Electric as D6883 in November 1963 and had a nomadic existence beginning in South Wales, then in Scotland, north east England before going to Spain in 2001. It returned to the UK in late 2012 and was sold to Europhoenix the following year and has been on hire to Rail Operations Group since November 2015. In May 2018 it was named *Cepheus* with the image of that star constellation on the left-hand side of the nameplate.
Keith Partlow

Colas Class 70 3,800hp diesel-electric 70811 heads the 14.05 Aberdeen Waterloo-Irvine Caledonian paper mill working through Stonehaven on Wednesday 3rd July. It was built by General Electric in January 2017, the first of a second batch of seven Class 70s ordered by Colas.

Richard Davies

Following a four-month closure due to a landslip near Baildon station necessitating major work to stabilise an embankment, services were restored to the Guiseley-Shipley line on 30th June. On Tuesday 9th July Northern Class 331/0 CAF Civity three-car EMU 331008 was at Baildon with the 14.21 Ilkley-Bradford Forster Square. *Chris Powell*

Rail Operations Group Class 37/6 37601 *Perseus* nears journey's end as it drifts downgrade through Llansamlet in east Swansea heading 7W79 the 10.25 Longsight Car.MD-Landore TMD on Tuesday 9th July. In the consist was former Transport for Wales Class 175 Coradia DMU 175111, Landore-bound for dilapidation works, with Europhoenix Class 37/2 37218 at the rear. 37601 was one of the first batch of English Electric Type 3s entering service as D6705 in January 1961 and has been renumbered four times, to 37005 in 1974, 37501 in 1986, 37601 in 1995 and back to 37501 in March 2025. It was purchased by Europhoenix in February 2017 and hired to ROG later in that year when it was repainted with the large Rail Operations Group branding applied by the side of the Europhoenix logo on the bodyside and was named *Perseus* with the image of that star constellation on the left-hand side of the nameplate.

Stephen Miles

Viewed from the top of Newcastle Castle Keep from where there is a wonderful view of the east end crossings at Newcastle Central. On Wednesday 10th July a TransPennine Express Class 802 Hitachi five-car bi-mode was departing south over Robert Stephenson's High Level bridge with the 10.43 Newcastle-Liverpool. The bridge which was completed in 1849 was stipulated in the enabling Parliamentary Act to carry both a road and railway line with the latter running above the road to reduce the width of the structure. It has six 125 feet spans carried on five masonry piers with the railway 120 feet above the river's high-water level.
Mike Robinson

Viewed from the 12th century Newcastle Castle Keep, a Lumo Class 803 Hitachi EMU was approaching Newcastle station with the 09.24 Edinburgh-Kings Cross on Wednesday 10th July. The service called only at Morpeth and Newcastle and was scheduled to arrive in London at 13.47. The large car park on the right was once occupied by station platforms. *Mike Robinson*

The era of Class 507 PEP EMU operation on Merseyside came to an end in mid-2024. In July there were generally two or three six-car sets operating on the Southport line each day to provide extra capacity because eight-car Class 777 sets were then not able to operate on that route; the Merseyrail system was otherwise Class 777-operated. 507017 was at the front of a six-car set into Brunswick heading for Southport during the evening peak period on Wednesday 10th July. *Darren Martin*

Northern Class 333 CAF four-car EMU 333005 arrives at Saltaire on Friday 12th July with the 12.47 Skipton-Leeds service. The units were originally built as three-car units with a fourth car added between 2000 and 2003; all were refurbished in 2019/20. Saltaire station, which is 3½ miles north of Bradford Forster Square, is uniquely located in a world heritage site.
Chris Powell

GB Railfreight reintroduced Brush Class 60 haulage to some Rylstone quarry services in mid-2024. On Monday 15th July Class 60 60087 *Ingleborough* was approaching Gascoigne Wood Junction with the 08.50 Rylstone-Hull Dairycoates loaded hoppers. *Ingleborough* is its third different name and was applied in April 2024 on a 1960s style Class 44 Peak nameplate. Now over thirty-years old, 60087 was sold by DB Schenker in March 2014 to Colas Rail and was purchased from them by GBRf in 2018. *Steve Batty*

New units of Greater Anglia's Bombardier Class 720 Aventra EMU fleet continued to enter service during 2024 with the final few appearing in early 2025. 720137 and 720140 at Ipswich on Wednesday 17th July were working the 12.14 Ipswich Yard-Colchester Up Passenger Loop TCMS test run. They arrived as the 10.42 from Liverpool Street and returned to Ipswich on the 14.48 from Colchester before working the 15.19 Ipswich-Liverpool Street.
Keith Partlow

After the withdrawal of the Northern Rail Class 319 EMUs on the Blackpool-Liverpool route they have been replaced by Class 331CAF Civity EMUs. Their superior acceleration apparently often requires the guard to reassure passengers at Euxton Balshaw Lane that "there is no problem with the train, we are a few minutes early waiting our time". Four-car unit 331110 carrying the name *Proud To Be Northern* was slowing for the stop at Balshaw Lane with the 15.05 from Blackpool North to Liverpool Lime Street on Friday 19th July. The 52.6-mile journey was scheduled to take 1 hour 17 minutes with stops also at Poulton-le-Fylde, Preston, Leyland, Wigan, St. Helens and Huyton. *Stewart Leyland*

On Sunday 21st July the Branch Line Society operated a rail tour from Birmingham International to Swindon, outward via Worcester and Oxford with the return going via Gloucester and then up the Lickey incline back to International, worked throughout by preserved Class 52 Western diesel-hydraulic D1015 *Western Champion*. D1015 was passing through the rarely used platform 1 at Bromsgrove. From building in January 1963 until November 1965 it had a golden ochre livery which was proposed by the late Brian Haresnape as an alternative to the standard British Railways diesel green but was not taken up, with *Western Champion* remaining the sole example although the Western class were all eventually painted in maroon. In 1979, D1015 was rescued, literally at the final hour before it was due to be cut up at Swindon, by the Diesel Traction Group. It was in appalling condition and after many years' effort and following what amounted to virtually a complete rebuild, *Western Champion* was restored to main line condition by 2002 and has worked extensively on rail tours since then. It never wore the blue livery with small yellow panels when in BR service and went straight from maroon to blue with full yellow ends.

Paul Chancellor

A long way off its beaten track, Transport for Wales Class 231 Stadler FLIRT four-car diesel-electric DMU 231004 passed through Hythe (Colchester) on Monday 22nd July working the 04.35 Cardiff Canton-Clacton CSD. It was going to Stadler's new facility at Clacton for attention to its bogies.
Keith Partlow

Motorists on the northbound A453 get a spectacular view over East Midlands Gateway rail terminal, which is cut into the hillside deep below the road. Catching a locomotive at that end of the terminal is tricky though, as they immediately detach from arriving trains and run to the far end. DB Cargo Class 66 66074 had just done that after arriving there on Thursday 1st August, and unloading of its train had already commenced. This view will disappear in time with the new trees planted on the embankment. *Darren Martin*

Southern Class 377 Electrostar dual-voltage EMUs 377456 and 377215 depart from the seaside terminus of Littlehampton with the 15.12 to London Victoria on Friday 2nd August. They were passing the London Brighton & South Coast Railway Grade II-listed 1886-built signal box which fringes Arundel and controls the immediate station area, including access to the carriage cleaning facility. The five-car units are not normally seen in passenger service outside of the suburban area although *The Railway Observer* reported sightings of the Class 377s on the Littlehampton service in July.

Graham Jelly

Transport for Wales Class 197 CAF Civity three-car DMU 197118 calls at Abergavenny with the 10.30 Manchester Piccadilly-Cardiff Central on Monday 5th August. Work was underway to provide step-free access at this station.

Steve Burdett

With only two months left in service before Royal Mail ended the contract from 10th October, Class 325 325014 was leading 325007 and 325001 with a postal service from Daventry to Shieldmuir depot in Scotland past Sytch Lane, Mill Meece north of Stafford on Tuesday 6th August. DB Cargo operated the trains for Royal Mail and the decision was made to withdraw them due to the ageing Class 325 fleet and the increasing costs of running electric traction despite Royal Mail praising their excellent performance over the years. *Peter Fogarty*

On Tuesday 6th August, a new Avanti West Coast Class 807 Hitachi Evero seven-car EMU 807001 was on a training run from Crewe to Oxley Carriage Sidings passing Sytch Lane at Mill Meece, a short distance north of Stafford on the West Coast Main Line. The first two Class 807s were accepted by Avanti in September.
Peter Fogarty

Freightliner Class 90 electrics 90011 and 90012 working the 02.10 Trafford Park-Felixstowe North intermodal service pass through Marks Tey, just south of Colchester, on Thursday 8th August.

Keith Partlow

Temporarily transferred to the Core Valley Lines (CVL) for the duration of the Welsh National Eisteddfod in Pontypridd, Transport for Wales Class 231 Stadler FLIRT diesel-electric DMU 231008 was passing Pontypridd North Junction on Friday 9th August when working the 14.08 Merthyr Tydfil-Cardiff Central-Aberdare. With limited parking available in the town centre visitors were encouraged to travel by train or use one of the bus-based park and ride services provided. In expectation of the large numbers expected to travel by train, TfW amended a number of its normal two-car Class 150 diagrams on the service to four-car Class 231s transferred from the Rhymney valley for the week. Pontypridd station and its approach lines have not been electrified as part of the CVL works and the catenary support merely carries electric cabling. *Stephen Miles*

On a beautiful Sunday 11th August, Direct Rail Services Class 66/4 66425 *Nigel J Kirchstein 1957-2021* was approaching Drem station with the SO 4E65 Mossend Up Yard-South Bank Tees Dock (DRS) Tesco containers. The train was slowing to go into Drem Up loop to allow several express trains to overtake it. Note the obligatory empty first wagon! *Keith Sanders*

The masts of *HMS Warrior* form the backdrop to this view at Portsmouth Harbour station. On Monday 12th August, South Western Railway Class 444 Siemens Desiro five-car EMU 444026 at the front of a ten-car set departs from platform 3 with the 12.15 to London Waterloo via Petersfield. SWR operates 45 of the twenty-year old Class 444 units and all were refurbished from 2017 onwards. *Graham Jelly*

DB Cargo Class 67 67022 was working the 18.55 Cardiff Central-Manchester Piccadilly service crossing St. Julian's bridge at Newport on Monday 12th August. The locomotive is one of just two black-liveried Class 67s leased to Transport for Wales for their 'Premier Services' to carry a matching livery for the former Grand Central Mk.4 sets acquired by Transport for Wales. *Richard Davies*

East Midlands Railway Class 222/1 five-car Meridian DMU 222103 after arrival at Sheffield with the 10.02 from St. Pancras on Tuesday 13th August. After 36 minutes allowed for cleaning, it formed the 12.37 back to St. Pancras. The Meridians will be replaced from 2025 by new Class 810 Hitachi Aurora bi-modes which began testing during the year. *John Jennison*

Northern Trains Class 195/0 CAF Civity two-car DMU 195007 arrives at Sheffield on Tuesday 13th August 2024 with the 11.39 Leeds to Lincoln Central which will reverse there for the continuation of its journey to Lincoln.

John Jennison

TransPennine Express Class 185 Siemens Desiro DMUs, 185140 and 185130, after arrival at Sheffield with the 11.23 Cleethorpes-Liverpool Lime Street on Tuesday 13th August 2024. It departed four minutes late and did not make up time, reaching Liverpool four minutes late.

John Jennison

On Saturday 17th August, West Midlands Trains Class 196/1 CAF Civity four-car DMU 196103 passes Severn Bridge Junction signal box on its arrival at Shrewsbury with a service from Birmingham New Street. On the left, a pair of Class 153 single units and two Class 196/0 two-car units were stabled in Abbey Foregate sidings. The three-storey high Grade II-listed signal box which was built by the L&NWR in 1904 is the second largest working mechanical box in the world with its original tumbler frame containing 180 levers, of which 89 are still used today. *Peter Fogarty*

Deep in the Black Country at Rowley Regis, DB Cargo Class 66/0 66055 *Alain Thauvette* had just breasted Old Hill bank with 6M96 Margam-Corby BSC steel coils on Monday 19th August, which had been diverted due to engineering work, and will be looped here to allow a passenger service to overtake. 66055 was named after the man who developed rail freight services at DB Cargo until his departure in 2016. *Steve Burdett*

A timeless scene at beautifully preserved and maintained Settle station as Northern Trains Class 158 two-car Express Sprinter DMU 158870 departed on Tuesday 20th August with the 13.36 Carlisle-Leeds.

Chris Powell

Direct Rail Services Class 66/4 66431 *Kingmoor TMD* was passing through Perry Barr station on the outskirts of Birmingham with the 4E49 Daventry Tesco) to Doncaster Iport intermodal service on Wednesday 21st August. It had been named at the DRS open day at Carlisle Kingmoor on 6th July and is the third locomotive to carry the name after 66301 and 37688.
Steve Burdett

From April 2024, West Midlands Railway Class 730 Aventra EMUs were gradually displacing Class 323s on the Cross-City Line between Lichfield Trent Valley and Redditch/Bromsgrove. 730024 and 730012 were negotiating the sharp curve into Sutton Coldfield station on Wednesday 21st August with the 12.05 Lichfield Trent Valley-Bromsgrove. The Class 730s first entered service with West Midlands Trains on 12th February and the Class 323s operated their last diagrams in public service in the West Midlands on Friday 27th September. *Steve Burdett*

Engineering work at Landor Street Junction, Birmingham saw a number of services diverted over the Cross-City line. CrossCountry Bombardier-built Class 220 Voyager DMUs 220019 and Class 221 221128 were rounding the sharp curve at Sutton Coldfield with the 08.07 Edinburgh-Plymouth on Wednesday 21st August. On 23rd January 1955, a diverted York-Bristol express exceeded the speed limit here whereby the train was derailed with 17 fatalities and 25 injured; the canopies on platform 1 were demolished. *Steve Burdett*

Europhoenix Class 37/4 37407 *Blackpool Tower* in British Rail large logo livery and Class 37/9 37901 *Mirrlees Pioneer* at Peterborough on Wednesday 21st August were working the 06.26 North Blyth-Wembley Rec hauling four KFA flats. 37407, one of the last Type 3s built by English Electric, entered traffic in October 1965, was privately purchased for preservation in 2008 but was subsequently sold to Direct Rail Services in 2015 and then to Europhoenix in April 2024. 37901 was the first of four Class 37s converted in 1986 to test the Mirrlees MB275T engine for the proposed Class 38. It was built by English Electric as D6850 in 1963 and was purchased for preservation after withdrawal in 1998 and then sold to Colas in 2016, but never used, and was purchased by Europhoenix and after an extensive overhaul returned to the network in June 2022. To the right DB Cargo Class 66/0 66047 *Maritime Intermodal Two* was waiting at the head of the 19.54 empty boxes to Dollands Moor. *Keith Partlow*

Engineering work at Landor Street Junction in Birmingham saw a number of services diverted in August. Colas Class 70 70816 with 6M40 Westbury-Yard to Cliffe Hill Stud Farm was passing Stourbridge Junction on Wednesday 21st August on a service that would normally have been routed via Banbury and Small Heath.

Steve Burdett

Taken south of the site of the old station which was closed in 1965 and was situated beyond the Lockhurst Lane overbridge in the background at Foleshill, a northern suburb of Coventry, Class 196 CAF Civity two-car DMU 196012 was working the 14.30 from Nuneaton to Coventry on Friday 23rd August. *Derek Huntriss*

On Monday 26th August a special timetable for CrossCountry's services was in force due to engineering works just north of Birmingham. At Derby, Class 221 Super Voyager five-car DMU 221134, having travelled via Lichfield with the 05.24 Plymouth-Edinburgh had a 30-minute wait. Meanwhile, a Class 170 TurboStar was arriving with the 09.53 from Coleshill Parkway.

Graham Jelly

GB Railfreight Class 66/7 66763 *Severn Valley Railway* at March West Junction on Thursday 29th August was working the 10.16 York Thrall-Whitemoor conveying four pristine Rail Head Treatment Train sets ready for the approaching season. 66763 was one of the last Class 66s built, entering service in late 2014 and was constructed by Progress Rail at Muncie, Indiana following the closure of the General Motors EMD London plant in Canada.

Keith Partlow

Avanti West Coast Class 390/0 nine-car Pendolino 390008 with the 11.50 Blackpool-Euston was passing through Berkswell, between Birmingham International and Coventry, on Thursday 29th August.

Derek Huntriss

London Northwestern Railway Class 350/3 Desiro EMU 350371 arrives at Berkswell with the 14.36 stopping service from Birmingham New Street to London Euston via Northampton on Thursday 29th August.

Derek Huntriss

In April 2019, DB Cargo Class 66 66109 was repainted into blue livery with PD Ports and DB decals applied. It was then named *Teesport Express* on 25th April and shortly afterwards took up the Tees Dock to Mossend and return intermodal circuit. Five years later, on Saturday 31st August it was back on that circuit passing Prestonpans station with 4E98 from Mossend Euroterminal to Tees Dock BSC Export Berth. Note on the right, the murals of local Prestonpans scenes painted on the old station building. *Keith Sanders*

GB Railfreight Class 69 69012 *Falcon 2* at Downham Market, between King's Lynn and Ely, on Monday 2nd September working the 12.26 Middleton Towers-Goole Glassworks loaded sand. It has been painted in an imitation of the two-tone livery carried by the Brush 2,700hp diesel-electric prototype D0280 *Falcon* between 1965 and 1970. 69012 was converted from Class 56 56077 and entered service in May and also has replica cast badges as fitted to D0280. *Keith Partlow*

Viewed from the elevated vantage point of the soon to be removed temporary footbridge at the eastern end of Selby station, Hull Trains' 15.08 Hull-Kings Cross, formed from a pair of Class 802 Hitachi bi-mode units with 802303 *Land of Green Ginger* leading 802301 *Amy Johnson*, were crossing Selby swing bridge on Tuesday 3rd September. A study published in February 2025 revealed that the open access operator, celebrating its 25th anniversary this year, saw revenue on journeys from London to Selby, Howden, Brough and Hull increase by nearly 300% in its first ten years. More recently, Hull Trains had passenger journey growth of 42% since 2018/19, 25% more than any other UK rail operator.

Bob Hayes

One of the last East Coast Main Line services not to be operated by Class 800 Azuma units is the single daily through service between Skipton and Kings Cross and the evening return working. On Wednesday 4th September this diagram was powered by Class 91 91130 *Lord Mayor of Newcastle*, at the head of the 06.56 Skipton-London Kings Cross, pictured pausing at Shipley, shortly after sunrise. *Julien King*

South Western Railway operates the majority of passenger services at Weymouth. However, the original station was built by the GWR and appropriately, taking centre stage on Monday 9th September was the current GWR's Class 166 three-car diesel-hydraulic Networker Turbo 166209. It had worked in from Gloucester and was waiting to take out the 17.28 to Bristol Temple Meads. *Graham Jelly*

LNER A4 4-6-2 60007 *Sir Nigel Gresley* at Ais Gill with the Carlisle-Hellifield-Chester "Fellsman" on Wednesday 11th September. 60007 was purchased for preservation after withdrawal in 1966 and was restored at Crewe Works using the wheels from 60026 *Miles Beevor* which were in better condition than its own. It was repainted in Garter blue and renumbered back to its original 4498 and worked on the main line until BR's steam ban in August 1968 and subsequently after the ban was relaxed in 1972. 60007 was in BR blue livery as photographed here from September 1950 until April 1952 and would have worked with crimson and cream coaching stock during that period. *Ian Pilkington*

On Friday 13th September Bombardier Class 378 Capitalstar dual-voltage EMU 378256 waits to leave from Clapham Junction's platform 1 with the 07.57 London Overground service to Stratford. The 17.6-mile journey was scheduled to take one hour and four minutes with 21 stops, running over the West London Extension line to Kensington Olympia and the West London line to Willesden Junction. *Richard Vitler*

Direct Rail Services Class 68s 68033 *The Poppy* and 68017 *Hornet* pass through Otford, with the 16.05 Dungeness to Crewe nuclear flask working on Wednesday 18th September. It will travel via Swanley, Shortlands, Catford to Clapham High Street and then over the West London line to join the West Coast Main Line at Willesden. *Rodney Lissenden*

66651 is one of the Class 66s converted by DB Cargo with a Higher Tractive Effort. Originally 66221, it was easing into Hereford for a crew change on the 09.31 Dee Marsh-Margam empty steels on Wednesday 18th September.

Steve Burdett

GB Railfreight Class 69s 69005 *Eastleigh* with 69012 *Falcon 2* on the rear at Thurston on Thursday 19th September working the 12.39 Stowmarket DGL-Whitemoor RHTT shakedown run. 69005 is sporting a livery based on that used for the Southern Region BRC&W Type 3s (Class 33) when built. *Keith Partlow*

Llanelli`s new £6.3 million footbridge, part of Network Rail's 'Access for All' programme, overshadows and frames both the existing footbridge and Transport for Wales Class 153 single unit 153327 forming the 14.19 Carmarthen-Shrewsbury, via Central Wales, on Thursday 19th September. Due to signalling work between Swansea and Llandeilo Junction, Heart of Wales Line trains were operating to/from Carmarthen, rather than Swansea, between 16th and 20th September. *Stephen Miles*

There is a convenient hole in the scaffolding on the temporary footbridge at Lostwithiel station with space for just one photographer at a time. Superb late September afternoon sunshine shines on this new elevated scene as Great Western Railway Class 43 Castle 43093 *Berkeley Castle* and 43189 *Launceston Castle* arrive with the 15.47 Plymouth-Penzance on Thursday 19th September. On the right, behind the now-closed Grade II-listed signal box is an aptly named business, 'Brunel/Two', which is a local property developer building luxury homes and apartments and is based in the former goods yard. *Bernard Mills*

The new station at Ashley Down opened to the public on Saturday 28th September following a ceremony the previous day. It is currently served by hourly stopping trains between Bristol Temple Meads and Filton Abbey Wood, with the intention eventually to extend the service to the proposed new station at Henbury. The platforms are situated on the slow lines, which are also used by many services to and from South Wales such as Great Western Railway Class 166 Network Turbo diesel-hydraulic three-car DMU 166211 passing through with the 08.23 Portsmouth Harbour-Cardiff Central on the opening day. The station occupies the site of the former Ashley Hill station, closed in 1964. *Stewart Jolly*

One of the first batch of Class 70s built for Colas in 2013/14, 70804 heads through Carlisle station on Tuesday 8th October with the 12.52 Carlisle Yard-Chirk Kronospan loaded timber working. The same locomotive disgraced itself three days later on the same working when it failed south of Carlisle blocking the West Coast Main Line for two hours. *Chris Powell*

Running as 3A83, new 807001 was at Euxton returning to London from Preston on a sunny Monday 14th October. In the distance Northern Class 195 DMU 195130 heads north with a Barrow train. Avanti West Coast officially launched the Class 807 electric-only version of its Hitachi-built Evero trains into service on 11th November, enabling the operator to offer an additional weekday return service between Liverpool Lime Street and London Euston. The Class 807's formal launch followed a soft launch between London and Birmingham on 26th October. *Stewart Leyland*

Although Tata's Port Talbot Steelworks last two blast furnaces ceased making iron on 30th September they continue to provide prominent landmarks. Transport for Wales Class 197 CAF Civity two-car DMU 197049 forming the 09.10 Milford Haven-Manchester Piccadilly passed by the site on Friday 18th October. *Stephen Miles*

GB Railfreight Class 69 69002 *Bob Tiller CM&EE* in British Rail large logo livery at Needham Market on Wednesday 23rd October working the 08.47 Peterborough North Yard-Ipswich Rec flats move.

Keith Partlow

ScotRail Class 334 Coradia Juniper three-car EMUs 334021 and 334005 pause at Haymarket on Wednesday 30th October with the 16.20 Edinburgh-Milngavie via Airdrie and Glasgow Queen Street low level. Introduced in 2001, the 40 Class 334s replaced the 1960s Glasgow 'Blue Trains'.
Chris Powell

Hauling possibly the last 10.05 Preston Docks-Haverton empty tanks, Colas Rail Freight Class 56 56105 was crossing the nine-arch Lydgate viaduct which carries the railway over the River Calder at Todmorden on Friday 1st November. The tank trains were the last regular freight flow over this line.

Graham Roose

The RHTT season was clearly underway looking at the state of GB Railfreight Class 66/7 66719 *Metro-Land* with an equally filthy 66725 *Sunderland* on the rear at Stowmarket on Tuesday 5th November working the 13.30 Whitemoor-Stowmarket DGL RHTT maintenance run.

Keith Partlow

Fresh out of the Hitachi factory, Class 807 Evero seven-car EMU 807006 approaches Longniddry when on delivery to Avanti West Coast on Wednesday 6th November. The route was up the East Coast Main Line from Darlington to Edinburgh and then down the West Coast Main Line to Wembley Inter-City Depot. All under the wires but taking over 13 hours! *Keith Sanders*

Running some twelve minutes late, Hull Trains 07.53 from Beverley to Kings Cross was rushing through Hitchin with Class 802/3 Paragon Hitachi bi-mode 802301 *Amy Johnson* leading 802302 *Jean Bishop (The Bee Lady)* on Tuesday 12th November. The Paragon fleet all carry names associated with Hull. Amy Johnson the legendary 1930s flight pioneer was born there and Jean Bishop collected for charity in the city for over thirty years dressed in a giant bee costume. *Paul Chancellor*

Detail of the top of GB Railfreight Class 66/7 66778 *Cambois Depot 25 Years* shows up well when it was hauling the 10.35 Doncaster-Leeds Whitehall Junction infrastructure train through Welbeck, Normanton, on Tuesday 12th November. On the left-hand side of the scene are the remains of the former Midland Railway route branching off from Goose Hill Junction towards Wath Road Junction, and on the right is the location of the short-lived Welbeck spoil unloading point.
Steve Batty

South Eastern Bombardier Class 376 Electrostar EMU 376028 had crossed the eleven-track viaduct on the southern approach to London Bridge station and was about to arrive at one of the through platforms with a service bound for Cannon Street on Wednesday 20th November.

John Sloane

With the autumn colours still showing and, after an early winter snowfall, running about an hour late, GB Railfreight Class 66/7 66749 *Christopher Hopcroft MBE 60 Years Railway Service* was crossing the 17-span Gauxholme viaduct near Todmorden with the 07.26 Liverpool-Drax biomass on Wednesday 20th November. 66778 was built for Cross Rail Benelux but was never delivered and after storage in Holland was acquired by GBRf in November 2012. After conversion to UK standards, it entered service in June 2013 and was named in December 2019. *Graham Roose*

The light covering of snow on the hills provided a superb backdrop for East Midlands Railway Regional Class 158 Express Sprinter two-car DMU 158852 leading another two-car set as they approached Edale, on the Hope Valley line mid-way between Sheffield and Manchester, with the 10.51 Liverpool Lime Street-Norwich on Wednesday 20th November. *Ian Pilkington*

The snow-covered hills of the Peak District dwarf GB Railfreight Class 66/7 66723 *Chinook* as it approached Edale with the 6H73 Washwood Heath-Tunstead limestone empties on Wednesday 20th November.

Ian Pilkington

Dalston Western Junction viewed from Dalston Kingsland station was the setting for Bombardier Class 378 Capitalstar five-car EMU 378148 as it approaches with a London Overground service from Highbury & Islington to Clapham Junction on Thursday 21st November.

John Sloane

The apartments on the right of the picture have a grandstand view of movements at Barking station. c2c Class 357 Electrostar four-car EMU 357320 departs from there with the 13.10 from Grays to Fenchurch Street on Thursday 21st November.

John Sloane

The London Overground service from Gospel Oak has been extended from Barking to terminate at Barking Riverside. It was known locally as the 'Goblin' line from the initial letters of the route but was formally renamed the 'Suffragette Line' on 28th November as part of Transport for London's rebranding scheme for its Overground lines. On Thursday 21st November Class 710/2 Bombardier Aventra dual voltage four-car EMU 710270 had crossed the junction with the link to the Great Eastern main line to arrive at Woodgrange Park with a train to Barking Riverside. *John Sloane*

The junction at Woodgrange Park determines the routing of cross-London freights from the Tilbury line; the left fork is the 'Goblin' route to Gospel Oak and the right leads to Stratford and the North London line. GB Railfreight Class 667/7 66724 *Drax Power Station* was heading for the latter route with the 12.42 from Tilbury to Wakefield Europort on Thursday 21st November. *John Sloane*

On Thursday 21st November early afternoon commuters check their phones as Thameslink Siemens Class 700 Desiro eight-car dual voltage EMU 700026 arrives at Farringdon with the 14.37 St. Albans to Sutton via Wimbledon service, whilst a westbound Metropolitan line train stands on the right at the slightly higher-level Underground platform. The Thameslink trains change between third-rail dc and 25kV overhead when they stop at Farringdon. The station was the eighth busiest station in the country with 46 million passenger entries and exits in 2023/24. *John Sloane*

The driver of GB Railfreight Class 66/7 66730 *Whitemoor* had just applied power for the climb to Skipton on Friday 22nd November, with the 12.27 Rylstone Quarry-Hunslet Tilcon loaded aggregates hoppers. The hills of the Yorkshire Dales National Park dominate the background.

Chris Powell

Low afternoon sun illuminates Northern Class 158 Express Sprinter two-car DMU 158816 as it crosses Selby swing bridge on Tuesday 26th November with the 14.15 Hull-Halifax which will reverse at Bradford Interchange for the final eight miles of the journey. The swing bridge was built in 1891 for the North Eastern Railway by Nelson & Co with ironwork by the Cleveland Bridge Company. It has five spans, with one fixed span of 110ft. 6in. and the swing span 130ft. across the River Ouse. *Chris Powell*

Having just refilled its tender from a road tanker at the Brighton end of the station, Southern Railway rebuilt West Country class 4-6-2 34046 *Braunton* starts away from a very wet Preston Park station with the Bath Spa-Three Bridges return leg of the Saphos Trains organised "Bath Christmas Market", on the evening of Monday 9th December. It was built as 21C146 at Brighton Works in November 1946 and rebuilt in February 1959. After withdrawal in October 1965, *Braunton* languished in Woodham Brothers' scrapyard until 1988. It was eventually restored for operational use in 2008 and was first used on the national network in 2013.

David Cox

The Stadler tri-mode (electric, battery and diesel) FLIRTs entered service with Transport for Wales in mid-November, initially with two diagrams on the Aberdare-Cardiff Central-Merthyr Tydfil service. This had increased to three by Wednesday 11th December when four-car unit 756117 was arriving at Aberdare in electric mode with the 12.38 from Merthyr Tydfil via Cardiff Central. The unit was passing the new 'set down' platform, part of which is visible beyond the rear of the train and was not then in use. It will only be required when the service is increased to a fifteen-minute frequency operated by the Class 398 'Tram Trains' starting in 2025. *Stephen Miles*

Father Christmas was waiting to board Northern Class 158 Express Sprinter two-car DMU 158817 at Ashington with the 12.17 from Newcastle on Monday 16th December. The line had re-opened to passenger traffic the previous day, 60 years after services were withdrawn by British Railway in November 1964. Marketed as the 'Northumberland Line', there are two trains in each direction every hour, initially with only one stop at Seaton Delaval, and with another four intermediate stations to be opened in 2025. Over 50,000 passenger journeys were made in the first month of operation.
Ian Pilkington

The Tyne & Wear PTE Metro network was opened between August 1980 and March 1984, running mostly on lines which were formerly part of the Tyneside Electric 600V dc system developed initially by the North Eastern Railway in 1904 and completed by the LNER in the late 1930s; the Tyne & Wear PTE was rebranded as Nexus in 1996. One of the new Stadler Class 555 five-car articulated units 555021 draws into the Art Deco West Monkseaton station which had been opened by the LNER in 1933. The unit was working a truncated service from Monument to St. James on Monday 30th December, when cross-Tyne services were suspended owing to concerns about the structural integrity of the A167 Gateshead Flyover. The first Class 555 had entered passenger service on18th December and the fleet of 46 new units will replace the Metro-Cammell twin-articulated Metrocars which have been in use since the system opened in 1980. *Bob Hayes*

CURRENT TITLES IN OUR CATALOGUE AS AT MAY 2025

TITLE	*ISBN*	£
RCTS Recent Publications		
BR Diesel and Gas Turbine Prototypes	978-1-7391324-8-4	25.00
Modern Traction Loco Data, Vol.1 - Brush Type 2s	978-1-7391324-6-0	15.00
LNER Investment during the Inter-War Years	978-1-7391324-2-2	20.00
A Railway Journey around the Cotswold and Malvern Hills	978-1-7391324-5-3	25.00
A Railway Journey across South Wales during the late 1950s and 1960s	978-1-7391324-7-7	25.00
Michael Mensing – Railway Photographer Vol.1	978-0-9934908-4-2	17.50
Michael Mensing – Railway Photographer Vol.2	978-1-7391324-4-6	25.00
Both Mensing 1 and Mensing 2 books as a bundle		32.50
Observing the Railway		
Observing the Railway in 2022	978-0-9934908-9-7	25.00
Observing the Railway in 2023	978-1-7391324-1-5	25.00
Both OTR 22 and OTR 23 books available as a bundle		30.00
Locomotives of the LMS		
Raising Steam on the LMS	978-0-901115-85-0	6.50
L&NWR Locomotive Names	978-0-901115-90-4	8.00
The Stanier Class Five 4-6-0s Volume 1	978-0-901115-98-0	20.00
The Stanier Class Five 4-6-0s Volume 2	978-0-901115-99-7	20.00
Both Class Five books (Vol.1 and Vol.2) available as a bundle		30.00
The Stanier Pacifics (reprint)	978-0-9934908-0-4	22.50
The Patriot 4-6-0s	978-0-9934908-1-1	20.00
Both Patriot and Pacific books together as a bundle		30.00
The Royal Scot 4-6-0s	978-0-9934908-7-3	25.00
Non Series Books		
Plymouth's Railways	978-0-901115-91-1	5.00
THE JOURNEY 978-0-9934908-2-8 10.00		
Brush Diesel & Electric Locomotives 1980-2020	978-0-9934908-3-5	20.00
A Photographic Journey from 1980 to 2020	978-0-9934908-8-0	15.00
An Illustrated History of first generation DMUs	978-1-7391324-0-8	25.00
The GWR King Class 4-6-0s	978-1-7391324-3-9	25.00

Purchase via our website rcts.org.uk or alternatively by post from RCTS Sales, 16 Welby Close, Maidenhead SL6 3PY, For all orders please add £4.00 for postage and packing. Cheques payable to RAILWAY CORRESPONDENCE & TRAVEL SOCIETY please.

THE DIGITAL ARCHIVE

The Railway Correspondence & Travel Society (RCTS) has been publishing definitive locomotive histories, stock books and the like since 1935. As most of them are out-of-print, the Society has decided to reimagine them for the digital age.

The RCTS Digital Archive seeks to republish the content to suit different types of users, wherever they may be and whatever digital device they may use. It is possible to buy some of the material in traditional book form but the archive is mainly designed to support online reading and downloading. All items are also available as a download subject to a fee in some cases.

The RCTS Digital Archive is available to registered users. Registration is free.

Please sign in each time to view the collections.

Visit rcts.org.uk to view and register

SCOPE OF ARCHIVE

Locomotives of the LNER – Originally a 19-part series published in 1963-94.
Now available as eight digital book style versions.

The Railway Observer – The Society's monthly magazine, 1,004 editions continuous from 1928 to 2011.
All copies available as single items, as a year's volumes or by decades.

Locomotives of the GWR – Originally in 14-parts published during 1951-93.
Now available as three digital book style versions.

Locomotives of the SR/L&SWR/LB&SCR – 11 parts published 1965-76.
Now available as four digital book style versions.

Locomotive stock books – Printed at intervals from 1934 to 1983.

Coaching stock books – Bi-annual publication from 1974-82.

Locomotives of the LMS – These are of hardback books that are currently out-of-print.

Locomotives of the Great Northern – Four Volumes published 1986-92.

Individual locomotive histories, localities and traffic surveys are also available.

MODERN TRACTION DATABASE

The Railway Correspondence and Travel Society (RCTS) launched a new interactive web-based Modern Traction Locomotive Database accessible to all at locodata.org.uk. Please visit to register your interest.

The database contains details of every diesel, electric and gas turbine locomotive that has run on the national network starting back in the 1890s through to the very latest changes in stock each month. All renumbering, naming and disposal information is included along with each reallocation and explanatory notes where appropriate.

Its unique feature is that searches can be made by number, number range, class etc. as well as by name and there is a 'free text' search for disposal and preservation information. Additionally it can be used to find details of every locomotive allocated to a particular depot or combination of depots over any specified time period and search results can be downloaded as pdf files if required.

It has been developed using thousands of hours of volunteer time and is the culmination of the RCTS digitisation project which has also seen nearly every one of its books published since the 1950s also being made available for download along with every single edition of its house magazine The Railway Observer, now in its 97th year.